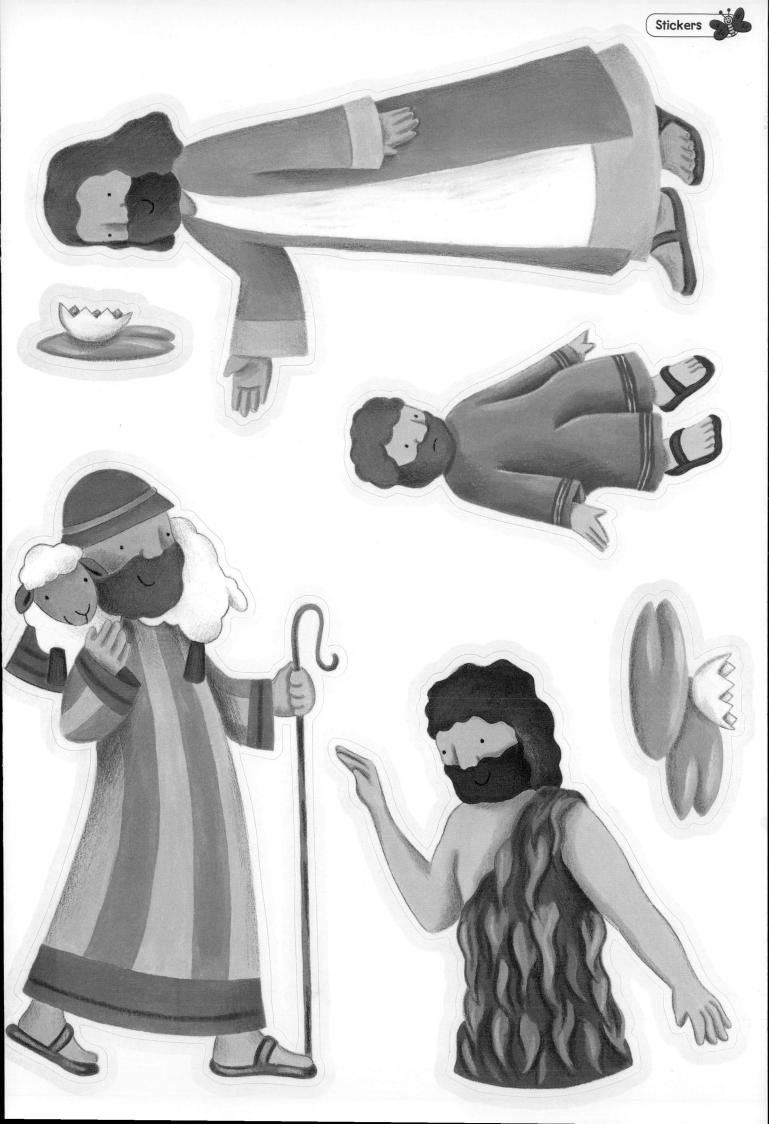

Stickers

AWESOME BIBLE ACTIVITY BOOK

CANDLE BOOKS

Paint or crayon the spaces without stickers.

Join the dots.
Put stickers where you see dashed lines: - - - - -

Use the chart as a guide to paint or crayon.
Put stickers where you see dashed lines.

1. Lemon
2. Light brown
3. Green
4. Light blue
5. Red
6. Light green
7. Blue
8. Grey
9. Mauve
10. Yellow
11. Light yellow
12. Dark brown

Bible Stories

Activity Fun

Adam and Eve are in the Garden of Eden.
God has told them not to eat fruit from this tree.
Draw some fruit on the tree.

Noah took two of each
sort of animal into the ark.
Draw a line to join the
pairs of animals.

Abraham is leaving his home.
He takes his family with him.
Put a cross through all the things
that didn't exist in Bible times.

Jacob gives his son Joseph a present.
It's a wonderful new coat.
Use your felt-tips to finish the picture.

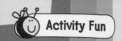

Moses is in the desert.
He sees a bush on fire.
Join the dots to finish the picture.

8

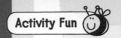

Moses leads his people out of the land of Egypt to the Red Sea. Which road will take them there?

Activity Fun

These twelve men are all spies.
They have been to look at the land of Israel.
Trace all the numbers from 1 to 12.

Samuel is helping in God's Temple.
He lights the candles.
Join the dots to finish the drawing.

David the shepherd loves to play music.
Join up the dots to find his musical instrument.
What is it?

David is throwing a stone at the giant Goliath. Which line must it take to hit the giant?

King Solomon is very wise.
He builds a new Temple.
Join up the dots to finish the picture.

Elijah is very hungry.
God sends birds called ravens to bring food for him.
Draw ravens flying to help Elijah.

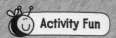

Daniel is put in a pit full of lions.
But God keeps him safe.
In each row of lions, one lion is
different from the other two.
Put a cross over the odd one out.

Mary has a surprise visitor.
Join the dots to find out
who is visiting Mary.

Here is Joseph the carpenter.
Draw circles around 2 saws, 3 hammers, and 3 chisels.

Mary and Joseph are going to stay in the stable. Circle all the things that are different in the bottom picture.

These shepherds are in fields near Bethlehem.
Join up the dots to see their special visitor.

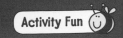

These wise men are riding to find baby Jesus.
Join the dots to see what they are staring at.

Now the wise men can see the town of Bethlehem.
Find 8 stars hidden in the picture.

22

Joseph, Mary, and baby Jesus escape from bad King Herod. Which road takes them safely to Egypt?

Jesus is twelve years old.
Mary and Joseph
take him to Jerusalem.
Which road must
they follow?

Jesus has come to the river.
John baptizes him.
Use crayons or felt-tips to finish the picture.

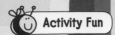

Jesus is telling stories to lots of people.
Join the dots to find out where he is standing.

Jesus is beside the sea.
He helps his friends catch lots of fish.
Use your felt-tips to finish the picture.

Activity Fun

Jesus invites Matthew to follow him.
Matthew collects tax money.
Draw a line joining the coins that are the same.

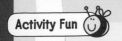

This good shepherd is searching for his lost sheep. Which path will bring him to his sheep?

29

This farmer is scattering seed.
Some seed falls among weeds. Some among
stones. Some gets pecked up by birds.
Draw in the weeds, stones, and birds.

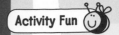

This boy left his home and family.
Now he wants to return to his father.
Which path will bring him home?

Jesus is sailing with his friends.
There is a fierce storm.
Draw the rain and some lightning.

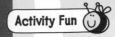

Jesus wants to reach his friends' boat.
He is walking on the water.
Which way will bring him to their boat?

33

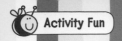

This sick man is being let down through the roof.
His friends want Jesus to make him better.
Draw in the ropes his friends use to lower his bed.

A boy gives Jesus his lunch
to share with a crowd of people.
Join up the dots to find out
how he carries his lunch.

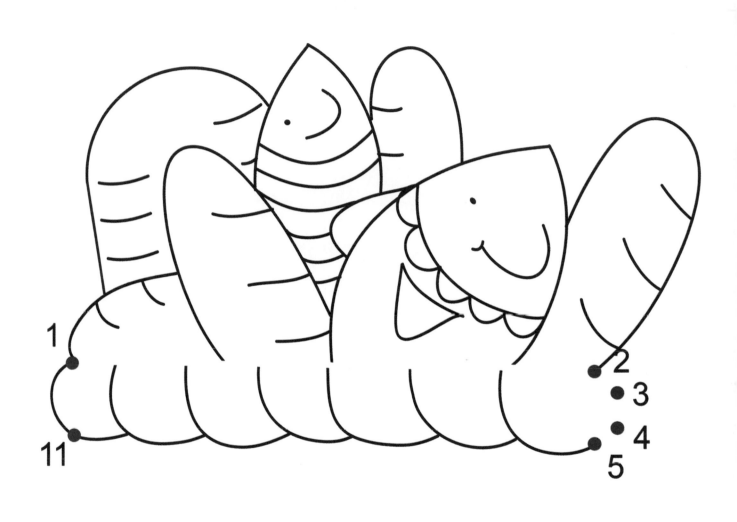

1

11

2

3

4

5

10

6

9

8

7

Jesus wants to visit his friends Mary and Martha.
Which road must he take?

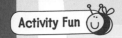

Jesus rides a donkey into Jerusalem.
How many palm leaves are on the road?
Trace over the numbers.

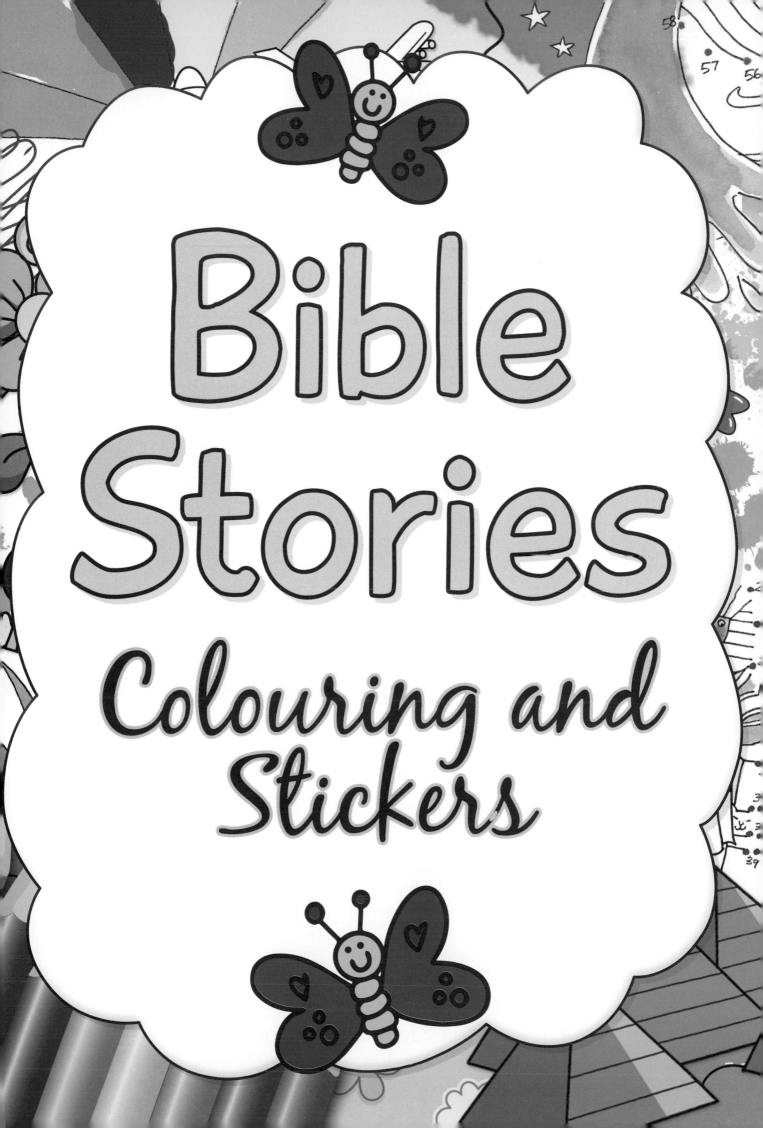

The princess of Egypt has found a baby boy.
His mother hid him in a basket, and floated it on the river.
The princess loves the baby.

**When he grows older, he will live in the princess's palace.
The princess names the baby "Moses".**

You can find this story in Exodus 2:1–10.

Jacob has given his young son Joseph a wonderful coat.
But Joseph's brothers are jealous.

"Why does Joseph get *all* the best things from our father?" they complain.

You can find this story in Genesis 37:2–11.

Daniel has been thrown into a pit full of hungry lions.
The king is amazed that Daniel hasn't been hurt.

That's because God sent an angel to shut the lions' mouths.

You can find this story in Daniel chapter 6.

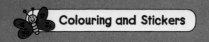

An angel has told Mary she will have a special baby.
She has married Joseph, the carpenter.

Now Mary and Joseph have to go on a long journey to a town called Bethlehem to be counted.

You can read this story in Luke 2:1–5.

Mary's baby boy has been born in a stable in Bethlehem.
She names her son Jesus, as the angel told her.

Mary wraps him in warm clothes. Joseph lays him in the manger.

You can read this story in Luke 2:6–7.

An angel has appeared to shepherds near Bethlehem.
"A baby is born who will save people everywhere!" said the angel.

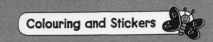

The shepherds rush off to see the baby!
They find Mary and Joseph in the stable – and Jesus lying in the straw.

You can read this story in Luke 2:15–20.

51

John has been baptizing people in the river.
Jesus comes along. "Please baptize me, too!" he says.

Jesus comes out of the water.
"This is my son!" says God. "I'm so very pleased with him."
You can find this story in Matthew 3:13–17.

Jesus finds two fishermen beside the lake.
They are mending their nets.

"Follow me!" says Jesus.
"I will teach you to bring in people instead of fish!"
You can find this story in Luke 5:1–11.

This shepherd has been out all night, searching for one lost sheep.
Now he's very happy. He's found his sheep!

He carries it back to the sheep pen.
God is happy too, when lost people come back to him.

You can find this story in Luke 15:3–7.

Robbers have beaten up this man and left him lying on the road.
The priest and the other man walked right past.

They didn't help. Finally, a kind stranger stops to help.

You can find this story in Luke 10:30–37.

When Jesus comes to town, everyone wants to see him.
Zacchaeus is very short. So he climbs a tree to get a good view.
"Come down, Zacchaeus!" says Jesus. "I want to visit your home."

60   *You can find this story in Luke 19:1–10.*

Jesus' friends are fishing on the lake.
Jesus cooks breakfast for them.
They are very happy because Jesus has risen from the dead.
You can find this story in John 21:1–14.

61

1. Lemon

2. Light brown

3. Green

4. Light blue

5. Red

6. Light green

7. Blue

8. Grey

9. Mauve

10. Yellow

11. Light yellow

12. Dark brown

Stories Jesus Told

Painting by Numbers and Stickers

NOAH BUILDS A BIG BOAT

One day God says to Noah, "A great flood is coming. You must build a big boat and put your family and every sort of animal into it." Noah does as God tells him. Noah's family and two of every creature are saved from the flood.

What does Noah see in the sky after the flood?

Find the answer in Genesis 9:13.

JACOB'S DREAM

Jacob is asleep in the desert, far from home. His pillow is a stone. In his dream he sees angels climbing up and down a stairway to heaven. When Jacob wakes up he says, "God is with me, even in this lonely place!"

Where is Jacob going?

Find the answer in Genesis 28:10.

65

THE KING'S STRANGE DREAM

The king of Egypt calls for Joseph.

"I dreamt about seven fat cows eating seven skinny cows. Whatever can it mean?"

"Egypt will have seven years of good harvest," says Joseph. "Then seven years with no food."

What other strange dream does Pharaoh have?

Find the answer in Genesis 41:22–24.

THE BABY IN A BASKET

The king of Egypt orders, "Kill every Jewish baby boy!" But one mother saves her baby. She puts him in a little basket and floats it on the river.
The princess finds the baby and takes him as her son. The baby's name is Moses.

What is the name of Moses' brother?

Find the answer in Exodus 4:14.

67

A VERY STRONG MAN

Samson is very strong. Once he killed a lion.
But enemies catch him. They take him to a great
party. They stand him between two pillars.
Samson pushes the pillars – and the whole
building falls flat!

Who are Samson's enemies?

Find the answer in Judges 16:21

RUTH HELPS HER MOTHER

Naomi is going on a long journey, all by herself.
Her daughter Ruth says, "I will go with you.
Wherever you go – I will go." So Ruth journeys with
Naomi to the town of Bethlehem.

*What is the name of
Ruth's husband?*

Find the answer in Ruth 4:13.

SAMUEL LOOKS FOR A NEW KING

David is a farmer's son. He plays the harp beautifully. God chooses this young man to be king of Israel. Samuel the priest pours oil on David's head to show he will become king.

What is young David's job?

Find the answer in 1 Samuel 16:11.

70

DAVID FIGHTS A GIANT

No one dared fight the giant bully, Goliath. David goes to the king. "I will fight Goliath!" he says. With his sling David flings a stone that hits the giant on his forehead. Goliath drops down dead. David's people rejoice.

Over which country does David become king?

Find the answer in 2 Samuel 5:3.

71

THE RICH QUEEN

Solomon is the wisest king of Israel. His people come to him if they have an argument. He decides who is right. Solomon is so famous that the rich Queen of Sheba comes all the way from her own country to visit him.

What presents does the Queen of Sheba bring?

Find the answer in 1 Kings 10:2.

RAVENS FEED ELIJAH

Elijah has run away to the desert. He lives beside a little stream. There's no food to eat! He grows hungrier and hungrier. So God sends birds called ravens, carrying bread and meat in their beaks. Elijah finds food in the desert.

Which king is Elijah's enemy?

Find the answer in 1 Kings 18:16–17.

73

DANIEL IN THE LIONS' PIT

Daniel has been thrown into a pit of lions. He spends the night there. But God sends an angel to shut the lions' mouths. Next morning, the king sets Daniel free. Daniel thanks God for helping him escape the hungry lions.

What is the king's name?

Find the answer in Daniel 6:25–26.

JONAH AND THE BIG FISH

Jonah is running away from God. He boards a ship. But a great storm comes up. Sailors throw Jonah overboard. A great fish swallows Jonah. Three days later the fish spits him out on the beach. God saves Jonah's life.

Where does God tell Jonah to go?

Find the answer in Jonah 1:1–2.

JOHN BAPTIZES JESUS

John lives in the desert. He wears animal skins.
"You must turn around. Stop doing bad things!"
he tells people. One day Jesus comes to him.
"Please baptize me!" he asks John. So John dips
him in the river. God is very pleased with Jesus.

*What bird appears after
Jesus is baptized?*

Find the answer in Matthew 3:16.

JESUS CHOOSES SPECIAL FRIENDS

Jesus wants a special team of friends. He walks beside the lake and sees two men mending their fishing nets. "Follow me!" he says. "I will show you how to fish for people."

What are these two men's names?

Find the answer in Matthew 4:18.

PHILIP MEETS AN AFRICAN

One day Philip meets a man in a chariot.
He comes from a country in Africa. As he
speeds along, the man reads part of the Bible.
But he doesn't understand what he's reading.
"It's all about Jesus," explains Philip.

*What does Philip do next
for the man?*

Find the answer in Acts 8:38.

PAUL IS SHIPWRECKED

Paul is on a big sailing boat. It's winter and a great storm arises. The boat hits rocks and starts to sink. "Please Lord, save everyone on board!" Paul prays. Soon every single person is safe and dry on a nearby island.

Which island do they reach?

Find the answer in Acts 28:1.

79

Here are Adam and Eve in the Garden of Eden.
What is Eve looking at? Read this story in Genesis 3:1–13.

Abraham and his family are leaving their home in Ur.
Read Genesis 12:5 to find out where they are going.

Joseph is a dream-teller. He's really good at explaining dreams.
Whose dream is he explaining here?

Read this whole story in Genesis chapter 41.

Samson is a very strong man. Enemies have captured him.
God helps him pull down this great building.
Read Samson's story in Judges 16:23–31.

Ruth is a kind lady. She cares for her husband's mother.
What is she doing here?
Read Ruth's story in Ruth chapter 2.

What is the old priest Samuel doing here? What's in his hand?
Read 1 Samuel 16:1–13 to find out. Who is the boy?

Elijah prays to God. What happens on the pile of stones?
Join up the dots to find out. Now read 1 Kings 18:20–39.

Join up the dots to find out what happens to God's messenger, Jonah.
Find the sticker for Jonah. Read Jonah's story in Jonah chapter 1 and 2:10.

Join up the dots to see how Joseph and Mary are journeying.
Where are they going?
Read this story in Luke 2:4–5.

Where are Mary and Joseph now?
What is Mary holding?
Read Luke 1:31 and 2:6–7 to find out.

Join up the dots to discover who Mary and Joseph find.
Where are they?
Find out what's happening here in Luke 2:41–52.

Who is talking to the Jewish ruler Nicodemus?
Join up the dots to find out.
Find out something important that Jesus said to Nicodemus in John 3:16.

Join the dots to find who's hidden in this picture?
What is he doing? Are the men in the boat surprised?
Read this story in Matthew 14:25–27.

Join the dots to find out who's holding the girl's hand.
What has happened to her? What is her father's name?
Read Luke 8:40–42, 49–55 to find out.

**Who are these men? What are they doing?
What happens next?
Read Mark 14:17–18, 22–25 to find out.**

Who are these soldiers holding?
Join up the dots to find out. Read Mark 14:43–46.
Who betrays Jesus with a kiss?

Bible Stories
Painting Pages

Adam and Eve look very sad. God sends them out of
the Garden of Eden because they disobeyed him.

Noah is filling his great ark with animals, two by two.

These men are trying to build the Tower of Babel. But they can't
understand each other, because they speak different languages.

Sarah and Abraham are so happy! They are both old,
yet God has given them a baby boy. His name is Isaac.

Joseph's brothers are very angry with him.
They tear off his beautiful coat and throw him into a pit.

Joseph is telling Pharaoh, king of Egypt,
what his strange dreams mean.

Miriam and her mother have put baby Moses in a basket
on the river. Will the princess of Egypt find him?

Moses helps his people, the Israelites, escape from Egypt.
He holds up his stick. A roadway opens across the Red Sea.

Moses' people, the Israelites, get very thirsty in the desert.
"Hit a rock with your stick," God tells Moses. Water gushes out!

Joshua and his people shout and blow their trumpets.
The walls of Jericho crash down!

God made Samson very, very strong.
He pulls down the pillars of this building. The roof falls in!

Samuel was fast asleep in the Temple.
Then he hears God call, "Samuel! Samuel!"

Sometimes King Saul feels very, very sad.
David plays his harp to help the king feel better.

The Queen of Sheba brings rich gifts for King Solomon.
She has heard he is the wisest king.

Naboth has a wonderful vineyard.
King Ahab wants it badly. So the wicked queen steals it for him.

Elijah is alone in the desert. He's very hungry!
God sends birds to carry food to him.

Daniel is in a pit full of hungry lions.
But he's quite safe, because God has shut the lions' mouths.

The angel Gabriel appears to Mary. "You are going to have a very special baby called Jesus!" he tells her.

These wise men bring rich presents for little Jesus.
What are their gifts?

Mary and Joseph search for young Jesus.
They find him talking to priests in the Temple.

Jesus reads from the Bible.
"These words are all about me!" he tells the people.

Jesus calls to Peter and Andrew.
"Follow me," he says. "Come and be fishers of men!"

Jesus finds Matthew, who collects tax money.
"Follow me!" says Jesus.

122

Jesus heals this man's bad leg.
Many sick people come to Jesus for help.

This poor man can't walk. Friends carry him to Jesus.
The house is full so they let him down through the roof.

The disciples look very surprised.
Where is Jesus walking?

This shepherd looks very happy.
His sheep got lost – but he's found it again.

This stranger comes along the road. He finds a man who is hurt.
He helps him – even though he's a stranger.

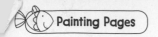

Jesus has died on a cross. These two men meet a stranger on the road. Later they realize it's Jesus. He's alive again!